John Sibley Williams' collection *As One Fire Consumes Another* transcends beyond the boundaries of family and history and country, beyond the body's tragedies, the "silenced bones of others." These poems rise as invocation, as testimonial to life's unfiltered beauty, violence, and faith, to the "light . . . already in us."

**–Vandana Khanna**, judge of The 2018 Orison Poetry Prize

*As One Fire Consumes Another* is a rare creation full of song and seethe. Though Williams' poems are composed of casket-like rectangular frames, their feral energy throbs against justified lines, creating vital articulations in a world where empathy is under erasure—where "even our ghosts have left us." His is a poetics of elegy and inquiry. These poems serve as witness to lives lost and interrogations of America's violence as well as its willed amnesia of that brutality. It is a book of radiance and ruin that manages to be benevolent while breathing fire.

**–Simone Muench**

If America's collective conscience is at war, the wounds and battle scars are in full display in John Sibley Williams' arresting book. No matter how dream-like, no matter how nightmarish or surreal, its startling landscapes reveal accurate truths about our country's dark humanity. Poem after poem, the strange elegance of *As One Fire Consumes Another* is remarkable and daunting.

**–Rigoberto González**

In the incandescent poems of John Sibley Williams' *As One Fire Consumes Another*, the suggestion of a collective *we* is another violence in a violent world where peace and war are suffered in equal measure. These poems live in brilliant little cages that Williams has built for them, the language itself held to the fire. This collection grieves. It flames. It says "your heart / hurts, and your heart hurts." I am in awe of the beauty and conflict, the elegance and restraint. These poems live in the merciless wilds of memory and tradition, where surrender means being consumed, and everything is made to burn.

**–Chelsea Dingman**

*As One Fire Consumes Another* is a guide through a troubled heritage and eventually death. Each sonic-rich poem places the reader in a different size coffin to watch life, making death always on the mind. Full of passion and heart, this book is always digging through the rubble towards life.

**–Tyree Daye**

John Sibley Williams indeed uses fire to consume fire, as his work's title enjoins. His poetry sets the normative uses of poetic language alight and burns away our safe skin of lyric expectation and contextual surety. At the core of this work, for me, there is not only the fierceness of fire, but the flow of blood. It is a poetry that does indeed "bleed the body of its language. Upside down above a trough, throat slit open at the name." Williams takes each of the ways his speaking agent knows others and knows the self, knows family and history, and physical wellbeing, and opens them to expose what has been denied, what is concealed behind the names we use as placation and false panacea. Do not expect to read these poems and be unchallenged, unchanged. While Williams manifests a speaking agent who is exquisitely culpable, courageously interrogating his lineages of human failings, a reader can't help but identify with what is the core of these crises. In that identification, I find how to enact for myself this kind of daunting journey, to walk into a fire and emerge burned and bled, and in that freed from living in denial. I will call this a work of recognizable revelations: not revelations that suggest serenity or imperturbability might be achieved, not revelations of how to leave our suffering behind. Rather it is revelation of compassion for others as well as for ourselves, in exactly who we are. From that comes an acceptance of the endless ache that is the human condition. As Williams recounts, one can come to a "dawn [of] burnt umber & all sorts of longing, one fire consuming another."

**–Rusty Morrison**

What is inside a box? The question is its mystery. Like an American Vasko Popa, Williams offers us a book of little boxes, "each one contained eternities and histories." If you reach into the dark of these boxes, what you find will surprise, enlighten and terrify you. One of the most original books of poetry I have read in decades.

**–Sean Thomas Dougherty**

These poems, clenched tight within a unified form, are the surreal dispatches of one mind thrashing against a larger American conscience that, in order to preserve its "sanity," must willfully ignore its unending thirst for violence. Time and again, through a kind of extended phantasmagoria, these poems illustrate how those countless acts of madness, seething just beneath America's surface, have been so casually ushered from collective memory, like how, "Blood washes quickly from the tile / floor."

**–William Brewer**

As One Fire Consumes Another

# As One Fire Consumes Another

JOHN SIBLEY WILLIAMS

Print ISBN: 978-1-949039-01-6
E-book ISBN: 978-1-949039-02-3

Orison Books
PO Box 8385
Asheville, NC 28814
www.orisonbooks.com

Distributed to the trade by Itasca Books
1-800-901-3480 / orders@itascabooks.com
www.itascabooks.com

Front cover art: "As One Fire Consumes Another" (2018), by Gary Hawkins.
Digital scan of ink on paper, 14" x 11".
Back cover art: "Matches, Consumed" (2018), by Gary Hawkins. Digital scan of
ink on paper, 7" x 11".
www.gary-hawkins.com

Manufactured in the U.S.A.

ORISON
BOOKS

# CONTENTS

## Keeping the Old World Lit

## We Can Make a Home of It Still

# ACKNOWLEDGMENTS

*The Adroit Journal*: "American Quanta" and "Places We Visit Once, & Never
Again"

*Angry Old Man*: "Errata," "The Children II," and "The Children III"

*The American Journal of Poetry*: "Dear Noah" and "*When instinct matures
into will,*"

*Arts & Letters*: "Everests"

*Asheville Poetry Review*: "Down by the Old Lynching Tree, a Flickering Light"

*Bellingham Review*: "Homescape"

*Carve Magazine*: "Everything Must Go," "There is No Such Thing as
Trespass," and "Understudies" (Winner of The Premium Edition
Contest)

*Cleaver*: "The Children I"

*Commonweal Magazine*: "American Émigré," "Another Story That Ends in
Cathedral," and "Here We Stand"

*concīs*: "July the 4th"

*Cream City Review*: "We Are Not Alone"

*December*: "Reparations" and "Toy Boat"

*Elm Leaves Journal*: "A Whole New Language to Unlearn" and "Book of the
Body"

*Figure 1*: "Instructions for Banishment" and "Minotaur // Dylann Roof"

*Green Mountains Review*: "Exile Says" and "Piñata" (Finalist for the Neil
Shepard Prize in Poetry)

*Greensboro Review*: "What My Mother Meant to Say That Night"

*The Indianapolis Review*: "Small Treasons"

*Juked*: "At the Wrist"

*Lake Effect*: "There Was No Heaven" and "The Show"

*The Los Angeles Review*: "How to Build an American House"

*The Minnesota Review*: "The Detainee Is Granted One Wish"

*Mudfish*: "The Crossing" and "We Are Already at War" (Honorable
Mention in 2017 Mudfish Poetry Prize)

*New Statesman*: "Daedalus // Oppenheimer"

*Ninth Letter*: "Homecoming"

*Penumbra*: "A Gift of Violence"

*The Pinch*: "Privilege"

*Poached Hare*: "I Sometimes Forget This Isn't About Us," "Us & Them," "Dear

*Poetry Northwest*: "Northernmost November"
*Portland Review*: "Boatbuilding"
*Puerto del Sol*: "A History of Skin" and "Sundogs"
*Redivider*: "The Invention of Childhood" and "Three Ways to Feign Suicide"
*Red Wheelbarrow*: "How We All Came to Be Here" (Finalist for the 2017 *Red Wheelbarrow* Poetry Prize)
*RHINO*: "Valentine"
*riverSedge*: "No Evidence"
*Ruminate*: "Grace Notes" and "Dear Jonah" (Finalist for the 2017 Janet B. McCabe Poetry Prize)
*Salt Hill*: "Lesser Beasts"
*Saranac Review*: "If"
*Solstice Magazine*: "Salvage" (Runner Up for the 2017 Stephen Dunn Prize)
*The South Carolina Review*: "Fallow as That" and "Field Confessional"
*Sycamore Review*: "Of Milk & Honey" (Runner Up for the 2016 Wabash Prize in Poetry)
*The Tishman Review*: "Sovereignty" (Runner Up for the Edna St. Vincent Millay Poetry Prize)
*The Tusculum Review*: "Harm"
*Water~Stone Review*: "Small Treasons" (reprint)
*West Texas Literary Review*: "Field Sermon: Reenactment" and "Field Sermon: Renunciation"

None of these fires would be lit without the unwavering support and care from people who have given me the gift of friendship and creative curiosity. My infinite gratitude goes to Anatoly Molotkov, Jeff Whitney, Sam Roxas-Chua, Paulann Petersen, Jon Boisvert, Samuel Seskin, and so many others who have kept this boat afloat over the years, as well as to new friends (and longtime inspirations) Sean Thomas Dougherty, Chelsea Dingman, Rusty Morrison, Rigoberto González, Dorianne Laux, Simone Muench, Melissa Kwasny, William Brewer, and Tyree Daye. Thank you. Thank you, friends.

The whole of my heart goes to Vandana Khanna for selecting this manuscript and to Luke Hankins and everyone at Orison Books for bringing this project to life. Thank you. Thank you.

And finally, my abiding and endless love to Staci and our children Kaiya and Gabriel, to whom I dedicate this book.

For Kaiya.
For Gabriel.

May you be lit from within by a different kind of fire.

# Instructions for Banishment

First line your threshold with salt. Shower your dead loved ones with insults to keep them from weighing down the cold half of the mattress. If you ever get around to sleeping again, don't dream heavenly. Stay close to bone, breath Breathe dust & bacon fat & whatever reminds a house that you are in it. Never forget that you are in it. Scuffed-up shoes & jeans worn at the knees; stop praying. Stop playing at prayer. Let everything not bolted down drift out onto the lawn with the first rain. Let it rust there. Leave timelessness to do with the past what it must. & with your body, & what's not entirely body. I know how hard it is to arrest a song as it crescendos to a deafening roar, then flatlines. Forget the lives you took, or failed to take. After all, we were at war, or a peace lasted too long. We are never really at peace long enough to suffer it. Wrap your fever in cheesecloth & wait for the throbbing to subside. It will never subside. I know regret is just another form of lust. Surviving your children is collateral damage. There is no end to *why*. There is no end. Throw some salt over your left shoulder. Cut the throat of every chicken in your neighbor's yard & bathe in their blood. Eat their hearts. Try on all sorts of silences until you find one that fits. Like a glove. Like a mask, a mansuit. Anything to hush the voices. Then never take it off.

# Harm

# Of Milk & Honey

To bleed the body of its language. Upside down above a trough, throat slit open at the name. Drop by drop, draining it of meaning, family, flag, & whatever home came before this one. Isn't that how it's done here? To tell a body *you are not my house*, then to furnish it with walls & fire anyway, with small semi-permanent objects that imitate a life, painted bottles packed with sand from some other shore. To live right on the shore & say *my body never crossed you* is one thing. To believe it is another thing entirely. Sure, my grandfather knifed your grandfather in the cargo hold of some vast ship heading vaguely west. But isn't experience merely what men call their mistakes? The rest is history or myth or rinse & repeat. We are an unsettlable people. To have made it this far yet still stare vacantly at our own hands like exorcised ghosts. To repeat into belief: *I have no home*, then to take it with us wherever we go.

# Exile Says

There is no escape, & no remaining.
The rhythm of the sea cutting ships
west toward newer old worlds, even
after weeks, can't rock you to sleep.
You know hope is a husked song, a
child slaving for an underground
factory, threads pouring through her
fingers into shirt & dress, yet you
hope. Exile says *at least I can claim
some small victory over ruin.* Days
multiply & your grandfather speaks
in your dreams of the cane harvest &
how his hands, back when they
loomed so large over you, softened
at your touch, then hardened again.
*Everyone needs a somewhere,* he
whispers, & since the dead have no
ears, you reply by listening. & there
is not much to ask of home but *why*
anyway. Why & how & if, none of
which are really questions. The sea
empties what it carries out onto one
or another shore. Exile says *at least
& at last & yes & yes!* & your heart
hurts. & your heart hurts. The cane
sways. Though there's no cane here,
it sways.

# The Children

Back when play carried less grief,
our darkness ruined only a half-acre
or so of the light. The rest was all tire
swings & spring-bound horses.
Leaping over cracks in concrete to
save your mother's spine. Weapon-
ized branches shaken loose by past
storms. Cowboys & Indians. Soldier
& Other. Then the world.

×

Do you remember when we cut eyes
into paper & wore yesterday's news
over our faces? How it took hours to
wash all that ink from our eyes. How
you would play one animal & I
would not-so-much-pretend to be
another. *Mask*, you called it. Then I
would ask *which one*?

×

There was a time we found stars in
our bodies. As I chased you across
the sky's absences. Rising: cresting:
falling, like any semi-permanent, lit
thing. Grass stain. Sprained heaven.
& me saying night contains so many
eternities we never know which will
hold us.

# Everything Must Go

Couch clothed in ghost-white sheets
like a fishing village in winter. Door
half-closed, just enough for the chill
outside to enter. Bed still clinging to
that new coffin smell. Bare mattress
with springs uncoiling, two indents
facing away from each other. A full
century pressed down on the gables,
all that moss & incomplete erasure.
There's a thrum in the unsung sky I
tap my foot to: out-of-synch always
with the dark drift of history. These
are not self-repeating tragedies; we
must sell off what we fear owning.
These are not hanging ropes, just a
few knotted cords heavying a tree.
Mine are not better bones. The glass
in the bathroom not mirror, exactly.
Our silence not atonement, my dead
parents either. For a good price, this
house & everything in it possibly
still on fire.

# Sundogs

*for Charlottesville*

This isn't how I'm told halos work.
Two mock suns lighting up the low
horizon, as if competing for grace-
giving, as if at war with each other.
The borders of their brief bodies
converging in one great arc flanking
then eclipsing the real. An imagined
architecture of virtue. A pure white
history. Torchlight flickers & feasts,
flickers & feasts, flickers & feasts.
Whatever we think they stand for,
the old gods are toppling.

# We Are Already at War

Once upon a time there was a story
not about desire or grief or wisdom.
Just a field beaten raw by summer.
Thigh-high grass graying like half-
healed stitches. No talking animals
to gently lesson us toward rightness.
No gods, grapes, reaching fors. No-
where to arrive or depart from, call
home or by cover of night flee with
what's left of your life. Son, it's not
always about more than survival.
That story never ends, until it does.
Close your eyes. Unhook me from
this impossible cloud you've hung
from an impossible sky. No, those
aren't great mythical beasts shaking
the earth beneath us. Those flashes
lighting up the night sky aren't stars
or fireflies. Close your eyes, please.
Sleep. Much of the burnt field will
still be here when you wake.

# Small Treasons

Somewhere, a body moves across
another without harm, as if taking a
knife to the sky, & we can answer
when a child asks where the world
goes when our eyes close.
Somewhere, we are sorry; I assume
for our silences. Bones ache & char
& must burn, somewhere. Even our
ghosts have left us. There must be a
place where hands aren't cages &
cages aren't gestures well-
intentioned but failing. Where we
love with more than body & hurt &
know when we have hurt. Some-
where, a less flammable history,
at least where the sparks fly upward
before falling back to ash.

# I Sometimes Forget This Isn't About Us

Then last night the neighbors' barn
burned down around two boys flush
with the exhausted calm following a
forbidden act of love. The language of
the town hasn't quite caught up
with the dark-skinned girl left half-
dead in the watershed, how it risks
the football team's winning streak.
Split piñata, the skull of the old man
whose register never held more than
a few hundred dollars. The *yes, we
can be better than this* chanted from
pews; the *some kinds of people have
it coming* added over steepled hands
each night before bed. The evening
news says something about a trailer
crammed with children overturning
on a desolate tract of earth bordered
by this & that country. Midnight, or
just after, our bedsheets tucked high
over our eyes, in no particular order
the dead return to us, palms open, as
if in apology, or self-defense.

# Down by the Old Lynching Tree, a Flickering Light

& a blindness. A dark silo scribbled onto night's thin skin. A young boy who often dreams of dying waking for a change to a soft voice asking how he's been all these years. & at the end of this vein of stars, a heart. A heart that bears too many shapes. A shape no farther from or closer to truth. What is the truth of it? The heart? The end? A brief rain feeds seeds & from nothing, if we're lucky, something we can hold on to, for now. Right now, somewhere in the world, a bird is thrashing the glass surface of a lake, coming up empty again. & a different boy, who often dreams of living into his teens, is mapping his road to the sky in metal shards held together by powder & fuse. A fuse he cannot light without help. A fuse he cannot light without fire. A fire that consumes the blindness. From the tired skin of night a rope snaps free from a burning tree.

# Everyone a History & a Context

*Whitney Plantation Museum, 2016*

Our entire country, as mapped on a
single body: for mapped, read *beat,
flayed, buried, forgotten*: for body,
read *a nameless hollowed out earth*:
for country, read *her home, & ours,
still*: for entire: *& still & still & still.*

# Say *Uncle*

In the dark of a man's fist pressed to chest. In salute to the older gods of *this is mine, also the rest.* Prayer, perhaps; the kind believers in prayer have forgotten, or fear can survive grace. Between any two bodies: a vacancy waiting to be filled. Give & take of blows. Unspoken agreement. In the drunk hours just before war.

×

The bell just goes on ringing. Not echo. Not metaphor. It's the steady hollow flesh-on-flesh that keeps us here. Each bruise contains eternities & histories. No, not always angst or cruelty. & not like sex, not always.

×

Surrender: *Uncle.* A body warring itself into manhood. A promise never to yield again. A planned kind of forest fire. All the hills inside are burning. The hills have always been burning. *I name the world: hurt. I name every body: body, every single fallen body: collateral: alien: mine.*

# Minotaur // Dylann Roof

*If you want peace, you don't talk to your friends. You talk to your enemies.*
    –Desmond Tutu

Left alone with your body this long.
No touch but carnage. No father but
a beast groomed for sacrifice. Like
the lesser gods before you, terrible,
hollow, utterly sincere in your need
for flesh between your teeth. It does
not matter that the labyrinth you try
to own owns you. No heroes in this
story. There have never been heroes
or villains in our story. Just want &
want & want &, in the end, a greater
want. An open-handed blow. Blood.
An unbroken church. Endless paths
tracing the same circles. Your skin,
untouched but by itself, becomes its
own motive.

# One Version of Events

Outside that handful of explosions
bright as white kites in a night sky,
nothing is alive enough to keep us
long on the long abandoned streets,
which eastward lead home & every
other-ward lead to different kinds of
rest.

×

From the unshattered windows, tiny
candle sparks stipple the retreating
shadows. Debris swirls about like
confetti. Dawn is burnt umber & all
sorts of longing, one fire consuming
another.

×

Tanned men in tan pants open their
bags as if in offering. Plastic bottles
& broad smiles. A thirst & water no
hands can cup.

×

We are looking for a night not yet
vandalized: an animal that need not
be feared: at least one fire that does
not burn: salvation without blood.

×

As dim stars cluster together & fall
silently over the hills, what seemed
unoccupied turns out to be a world

×

of tents & flags strangely becoming
less strange by the day. Negotiation.
New gods speaking in the same tone
as the old. Hope & undying pledges
to home. One body birthing another.

# Us & Them

Not that the alloy filament sparking iron wires needs us to call this *light*. Even in our absence, shadows flee, & when the switch lowers, return to us undiminished. Not that the dead won't still be here in the morning if we dress their wounds & declare the world healed. It's not that anything really heals. Not that torture works or fails. Even if they drown upside down in a small bucket of water in a white room lit by a single swaying bulb, our questions keep coming.

# The Detainee is Granted One Wish

From one broken country to another
: do you still pray to the gods we
fashioned from photos of our absent
fathers? All grizzle & spit, sky, fist,
love. You must have arrived here by
belief too, searching for something
you could mistake for a life. Back
when we lived in the house that had
nothing in it, did you think, even in
your wildest silences, another one
was waiting on the opposite shore?

×

If home is more than a body's ill
rapport with walls & wants, drones,
dust, rebuildings, & *never-agains*. If
escape is just another word for *yes, it
happens here too* & torture but a
failed embrace, a kiss too soft. If,
when they redraw the maps, joining
our skins into one world, one great
experiment in empathy, you beg me
for forgiveness; what if I apologize,
again, instead?

×

Nothing shatters, yet our voices are
made entirely of glass. Yes, nothing
stays, yet here we are in the same
small prison touching hands &, yes,
sharing breath. If this is our liturgy,
let there be so much damn smoke &
dance & flagellation & lovemaking
that our fathers finally recognize us.
Blood washes quickly from the tiled

floor. My sky opens to yours, then closes. When you sever the heads of certain beasts, they grow right back. This is how I'd like you to fail me.

# Hindu Kush

All the horizon's creases ironed out.
Hills flattened to field. Netting torn;
fish freed. Songs emptied of singer,
audience. Now the warred-against
have some space to study the why.
The valley weighs captivity vs. how
tenderly clouds collect in its belly.
The earth cannot hold itself still; all
this trembling. The chalk houses are
erasing beneath their families.

×

& all houses still standing began as
chalk outlines of former homes. The
dead, before that first breath, merely
a prayer for legacy, seed for a burnt-
out pasture. All mothers were once
daughters & all daughters know the
best method of preparing the earth
for their mothers. The earth cannot
hold us all inside forever. All skies
still believed in are grounds to kill.
All our paved roads lead to ambush.

# *When instinct matures into will,*

we can finally have a go at cruelty.
Sometimes I miss baring my teeth
without menace, from hunger alone
ripping into weaker animals, taking
only what my body demands. Feral
without being brutal, trembling with
all I have but cannot own. Owning
my hands. Owning the blood on my
hands. Never asking for forgiveness
& being forgiven.

×

Give me back the ache. *Six children
killed in Kabul* yet nothing stirs the
birds from our oak. The horizon sits
precisely where we left it. Fat with
faith. Fat, faithful, choosing what to
feel, feeling nothing.

×

Invent a story that ends just short of
its beginning. Raw & rural. Ache &
echo. As if we have ever been more
by being less. Immigrants beautiful
under stadium lights. Before that, a
small collection of losses. & before
there were things to lose, simply fur
& claw, gesture, consequence.

×

Bit by bit the bomb steals what no-
body has enough of to offer; offer
them everything, I tell my daughter.
When they come, revert to violence
without fury. Show your teeth, bite

down, & if you're full, release them
back to the wild, without mercy.

# Field Confessional

*for Zubair Ahmed*

Soon this winter field will be dense
with thawing bodies. Bloat & dust.
Raw bones rising up like old stone
wells from a dank & grassless earth.
Rope connecting them to the future:
frayed, nearly snapped. & no bucket
big enough to haul up what's been
lost. There is a way the snow has of
whitewashing what is already white.
Rote history, hands. Set for hanging
my sister's wet white dress & what-
ever else we didn't discard over the
long hardening months. Dog-eared
books, privilege, woodstove, maybe
regret. The window is narrowing.
Soon we will know these bones as
animal or human. I must confess I'd
be surprised if either survives our
forgetting until spring.

# No Island Is an Island, & So Forth

Sign your name to ruined Civil War
forts. Next time, use a Sharpie when
listing your demands to god. Instead
of touching forehead to ground as if
in supplication/ecstasy/grief, set fire
to the old battlefield & let the winds
unsever your strings to the past. In
dust & degrees, redraw boundaries.
This is what happened & this might
be what we let happen again. When
writing your obituary, make sure to
leave some space for grandfather's
casual racism. Keep stringing your
old tennis shoes over power lines &
don't heed the complaints of crows.
Testify against earth & sky alike.
Lost luminosity is a gift. Like tele-
vised violence. Like tectonic plates
scraping together, birthing islands.
No island is an island; no body just a
body, & so forth. When the South
rises again, carry your father with the
rebel flag tattoo to the window to
watch the burning. Let the world
laugh at itself. Break from tradition.
To men who want & want & want,
admit you've tried so hard not to be
one of them.

# No Evidence

*Texas says there is "no evidence" of wrongdoing after mass graves filled with bodies of immigrants were found miles inland from the U.S.–Mexico border.*

–Democracy Now, "Mass Graves of Immigrants Found in Texas," July 16, 2015

*There are basically only two subject matters in all Western culture: sex and death.*

–Peter Greenaway

Body atop body in some vague act
that might be called love if not for
the caption *Mass Grave Discovered*.
What I took to be mouths frozen in
ecstasy, limbs linked in lust, men &
women united in a heavenly gesture
I'd never know, angled slightly into
horror. The meaning we make from
things depends on the camera's eye.
I cannot see the undead stars surely
overhead, the white windowless van
abandoned nearby, faces reconciling
with their names, as I cannot see my
-self with all the mirrors removed, as
I cannot touch my wife when she
rolls to the window-edge of the bed.
Backlit by the teeth of border lights,
sewn into the hide of the landscape
like maps, dozens of officers shovel
up hundreds of loose fitting bones.
Parents & children & doubled-over,
sexless stars; all profanely beautiful.

# Harm

Bicycles abandoned in near-green grass. Baskets heavy with matches & bottle rockets, BB guns & hurt. Smoke from the munitions factory threads together with smaller human burnings. Our future closes in. Stars pierce the night inside the night inside our chests: dimly at first, then brightly as a long trail of spent fireworks.

×

Home: a cardboard castle softening in the rain. Landscape: closing in all around. Harm: as if acclimating to hurt. Hurt: imaginary, or otherwise.

×

Whatever *it* is, we need more of it.

×

We wait our turn to make others ache the way we're told god aches once the world has left him: wait for something larger than a stick to beat doors into a stranger's skull: wait & wait for that kind of entering: walk the barbed wire field past our youth into that overlit gymnasium where a solider gives names their numbers.

×

All we want is an honest storm to carry us forth. Something righteous.

Not another story of lost wings. Not
another body speaking itself alien.
All   our friends work the same fact-
ories as their mothers & fathers; all
summer the same sad sun burns up
the same fields. Harm: hurt: home:
etc. We are less afraid of the dark
inside than of all the light.

# A Gift of Violence

*It feels like violence is coming.*
       –Sen. Ben Sasse (R-Neb.),
       on Charlottesville, 2017

Memories of burning buildings raw
& righteous. A grandfather's flames
passed down, undimmed. A full set
of knives in the drawer without time
to blunt from underuse. A city never
quite white enough. A city furiously
lit by misremembered histories. Mis
-identified origins. Hands cleansed
in that well. That deep well out back
behind the house. That house flying
a failed flag, failing in the breeze.
There is a breeze here that carries a
hint of smoke from older crosses &
parents  who pray to hungering gods.
On a night this clear you can make
out the darkness around stars; torch-
bright, sincere, the darkness in our
stars.

# Homecoming

Goddamn the vacuum of a Midwest
winter, when even those hard winds
cannot tremble the withered wheat.
Goddamn the *what's-left-to-say* dry
& empty in our mouths after eulogy
turns too truthful. Rifle volleys that
shake out the last few hardy birds,
convince me. Drape me like a flag.
Shape me like a coffin. Imagine him
over there; burning sand, hard light.
Believe me the *why*. Goddamn the x-
rayed December trees, the bullet still
lodged in the skull of night, this
shovel-breaking earth we break &
drape in stars, stripes. Partisan hush
fat between us. Thank you, mother;
goddamn the rest. Let's call a body a
*body* & never by its name.

# Here We Stand

Pulleys and old ropes and held feet
above the floor, lowering, so many
crates cut to look less like men than
pomegranates shipped in especially
for this crowd of mourners to bite
into while holding their free hands
over their hearts. Blood orange rust
lines the green truck ferrying a flag
and my brother under the flag from
one end of our lives to the other. If,
under certain skies, our icons outlast
us, let this be one of those heavens.
Not the preached and prayed to, just
a brief and hungering silence grown
stronger in its breaking. What might
be said, so much less than needing to
say it. The father of our country is an
angry god, gutting youth from the
youthful, wood from the field for
bodies given back to the field. Rifle
clap. Contrails divide the sky. Many
smokes must meet to twine enough
rope for the dead to escape. And the
darkness, all the light still caught in
their mouths; we have no idea how
to account for its song.

# Dear Jonah

If you can imagine each rib a bow
sawing some music from the hollow
gut of a violin, then surely the dead
whale here rotting away in the sand
can be called rousing. Harmonic. In
a way, beautiful. Let's say the boys
fighting with our dogs for viscera to
smear all over the fresh white shirts
of girls they love are our saviors.
Grace-lights. Hand-me-down Army
boots filling with blood, their names
divided by hearts tattooed into trees.
Imagine the work it takes to rend
bone from bone. I find it difficult to
imagine what we'd do to each other
during times of peace. An arena fills
with refugees a few miles inland.
Power lines sag from the heft of
homebound calls. Without shrapnel,
your father's chest would simply be
another unplayed instrument. Let's
say we are playing our hearts out.
Innocent again, with that wide-open
belly of a whale calling us, finally a
death you can almost call song.

# The Crossing

Tell me what not to do with heaven-
faced children torn between parents
who are torn apart by a river tearing
a long muddy scar into this long &
lengthening landscape. Then tell me
again why we are the only animal
bound by maps, shifting allegiances.
Tell me what not to forgive of stars;
what skin my skin is forbidden to
touch; what heart my heart cannot
possibly hold without breaking.
Don't tell me the best way to break a
body without damaging the shell.
We all know how that story ends.
Ask the bridled horses. Ask mothers
waiting by docks for warships never
to return. Ask any long, cold winter
night in any part of any country any
child has ever fled to find herself no
closer to home. Please tell me what
road that begins in ruin ends
somewhere beautiful.

Keeping the Old World Lit

# American Quanta

*[W]e ourselves are a part of the mystery that we are trying to solve.*
        —Max Planck

We need new songs. We need a new
chorus for the songs our great-great-
grandparents sang beneath the same
stars that bore our country, suffered
it. The architecture of the heavens is
a small white farmhouse boarded up
for the winter; all manner of horror
& light shot through the old hanging
sycamores. & our hearts, if not our
bodies, still beat against the bowed,
bowing walls. In small eruptions of
knowing held up to themselves,
pierced by what our eyes take in,
translate, refuse. Grains of space fat
& empty, pulled toward & pushed
away from each other; new harvests
of the same cotton. Derelict barns
burn as fiercely as the ones we keep
our horses in. I don't know if theory
is the same as the cramps that ache
my hands when weather shifts or if
callouses are just synonyms of stars.
Before my name there were other
names, & after my name, the same.
The stillness in the windless treeline
should not be confused with inertia.
Interactional existence; when I look
at where we come from, it's still not
nowhere, or forgiven.

# Everests

Tell me of wheat bent by aliens
again. The thimbleful of truth in
every incredible story. How old
stones roughly dispersed over miles
of rough Spanish coast are remains
of a refuge. A once-mighty city lives
in my lungs. I tell people the world
is big enough for all our histories.
Troy and god and God, etc. Someone
I once loved enough to almost marry
but not quite enough to remember
her face confessed each night she left
her body for worlds where skin was
a myth, some fireside fable passed
down generations as a warning. A
once-mighty fire burns in my palms.
My children are learning all wars
begin with belief. Tell me what to
believe, Dad, and I'll kill whatever it
takes to keep us ~~safe~~ here. An eight-
legged monster for every sea. A
flood for every rebirth. Here is a
half-human bull for your maze; son,
believe it or not, all the tallest
mountains are underwater.

# If

If the entire field is held together by one pitchfork. If the dark torso sway of night trees puts our storied past in doubt. If us, then our negation of another. If light, then far too many shadows to count. If the russet dust kicked up behind a plow making its last pass at harvest began as a body burnt then blended with the earth. If the earth is a body & I am one of its persecutors. *Spine straight, & don't take your eyes off the barrel / noose.* Even if it fails, if tied just right, how rope leaves its intended mark. & if the rusty old pitchfork finally snaps & it turns out the field just keeps on going without us.

# The Bones of Us

*for TJ Jarrett*

Calmly, the earth opens. Erosion. &
the stray dogs are there in minutes to
pick apart, polish, drag home.
What's left is what's always left in
times like these. Clean white bones.
Hints of past glories. Ghosts of un-
forgiven horrors. Young cities dead
& ready for rebirth in our lungs. But
in the absence of lung, flesh, knife,
guilt, the children collecting us into
pails for study must make due with
our angst. Once it's tasted blood, a
sky never loses its red. Call it love.
Call it by its true name: schism. Dis
-unity. Before we were a country of
burning buildings & protest & want,
we were the same. A shining city on
a shining hill raised on the silenced
bones of others. They will find us &
ask what went wrong with the world
to make the present seem so distant,
alien, cruel. They will hold us high
as example, excuse, exhausting all
the usual metaphors for fire before
forging from our embers the words
to justify themselves.

# Piñata

Body broken into. All the sweetness
torn out. Brightly dyed paper flakes
linger in the grass as if someone has
sanded down the sun. The husk of an
animal hangs loosely from a sky
clouding over in storm. Tomorrow
he will be a man. Until then, sticks
are just sticks. Thrashing the insides
out of some martyred beast is play.
Lollipop. Marzipan. Tamarind. Fire
works its way up the arm into bottle
rocket into *bang*. The sky glimmers
& is gone. & whatever the children
can carry home in their teeth will be
theirs.

# Daedalus // Oppenheimer

All labyrinths, like those first fires rising over a red New Mexico sky, were intended to trap their creators. Even in their insatiable hunger, all monsters are scared of our conquest. When the lights go on & everything we've made flickers & flares & fulfills its promise, we find ourselves to have always been the scorpion on the turtle's back. The river is deep, inescapable. All our wings are made for burning.

# We Are Not Alone

In this, we are safe. At least bridges
similarly strain to meet both shores:
factory fires burn long after closing:
sycamores struggle to hold a nest of
eggs in their arms. Even the storms
that shatter us hesitate a moment, as
if in reverie, prayer, before making
us what we are. I am steadying his
body on an oak chair with one short
leg. I am setting a place for ruin at
the table between us. It's not his
weight that forces the fall, not food
that feeds him. All older versions of
ourselves, broken enough, break in
our care. & I still care what happens
to the bridge once there's no river to
span. I still burn, & night. As deer
don't call the slowest among them
*father* anymore. As the storm calms
without ever entirely passing.

# The Children

What began as dinner deconstructs into impossible questions, trembling answers. *No*, we cannot eat oceans, only what lives there. *Yes & no*, the stars never leave us, at least not for long. *Yes*, like love. Sadly not like beauty, or youth, or grandpa. I don't know what faith means. *No*, the war is not so far from here.

×

Through curtains of smoke. Bruise, mirror. Through your hands clasped over your eyes, as if skin could hold the world at bay. Through our hard shadows tossed against harder wall. Old & resewn flags. Night & still it is night. After all our mistakes, let's say we can return to whatever love was, before we named it.

×

Go ahead, write what you can't say aloud on my palm: on the underside of a ship before it runs aground: on top of that tiny X etched with huge hands a bullet calls course, purpose, & eventually, home. There must be room enough on the tip of a tongue for every imaginable silence.

×

Every scream fades to a murmur on

the wind: to nightmare, then rumor. The whole town is whispering about what took our parents great pain to realize, express, die for. Only after echoes fade can we hear what was being said. My only prayer: for your crosses to weigh so much less than hummingbird flight.

×

You teethe on old sparrow bones: on dreams hung loosely like bodies from star-tips: on the full sea-to-sea reach of an infant country hungry for more of itself. Yet you are still hungry, growing more so each day.

# Boatbuilding

And yes, we all learn to be boats  by
navigating our mothers' sleeping
chests. Calm sea of linen on lung.
Two tiny oars growing less useless
every stroke. And yes, our fathers
stand taller than a hundred masts yet
tremble when handed the frailest of
bodies. Their heavy silence is a net
dragging empty behind us. And yes,
we'll end up casting it all back to the
sea someday. Someday it will be our
turn to grieve, to distance. But how
close skin feels, briefly, now, as
we're learning its edges.

# Understudies

In our parents' bedroom exchanging
overalls for ties, bras. I am playing
mother again, and, Tyler, for those
ten minutes between breakfast and
church you can be Dad's hard open
palm. Both your feet drown in his
shiny black Sunday shoes. It takes
time for the world to whiten around
the temples, to scar. You are trying
and failing to find something awful
enough to pray away, stuffing your
big-boy pockets with miracles that
sound like stopped watches. Now
hold me how they say they held each
other once. Tell me how pretty I was
when your arms first danced my
waist around a crowded Elks Lodge
to a song that ended in two sons and
a need to atone. And I will show you
how to be forgiven without asking
the sky, how to love without using
your mouth.

# The Invention of Childhood

The day after I buried my daughter
in poorly-folded origami swans, koi,
cranes, roses, saying *this is how we
learn to fly,* saying *happy birthday,*
whiskey-warm I fell in love, finally,
with what I took to be fatherhood.
We were watching planes line up
along designated paths, one & then
another lifting & gone. She was two
& the world was golden & nothing I
said would stop her from asking the
questions I'd forgotten had answers.
Early morning stars stuck to the sky
like flypaper, snared, buzzing about,
nearly dead. Her paper animals, all
flightless, crumbled & spit-stained,
left tiny hollows in the snow. Plural
& alone, working my fears through
her hair, I sunk an angel into snow &
gave it her name; lit a cigarette &
another; cocked my finger at each
plane & at the stars, blinking out;
said *we'll always have next year* &
realized I meant it.

# A History of Skin

I've played out the Cowboy/Indian
narrative by myself in dark wooded
corners where trees hold each other
so damn tight the sky erases itself. I
remember beating my t-shirt against
rocks to get the blood out, how dirt
brown the stains set, how stone isn't
the best salve. Turn a switch around
& spear becomes rifle, son turns to
man. *Please bury me like this*, I said
to no one who could hear me. Gray
as bathwater, as the palette between
skins, one not really mine, the light
passed through a thousand branches
before failing to find me. I opened &
closed. If every good story begins
with a lie, this is mine: once a boy
who played both sides of slaughter
returned home with a bloody shirt &
thought that would absolve him.

# Field Sermon: Reenactment

Somewhere in the close darkness,
pinned to shadow, in the small hour
just before those delicate fires dawn
ignites in you take hold, a mule deer
steps into range and your father asks
*is this not what we've prayed for?*
and you answer again with a bullet
that misses its mark. Then morning
comes with its empty hands raised
overhead like surrender. Later, war.
Then another autumn with its trees
undressing into your mouth and that
sticky metal sleeplessness of having
learned, finally, to kill. Then there it
is: another boney halo of antlers, lit
from behind, though detached now
from a body's fire, a body's grace.
Another chance to make him proud.
Yet another breathy chant to no one
in particular. Your father is dead.
And his Father. The morning hung-
over from night. When you ask it, the
world gives you its throat.

# The Show

& so we go toward the show. Torch
lights barking bright, flint-struck &
falling embers everywhere. White
canvas steeples prop up the evening
sky. The dark dreams we once had to
shove under our mattresses now on
full display. Old deities spill across a
grassless field. A small box cranked
by a monkey dressed in its Sunday
best shakes loose some sad little
song. All the women are made to
look like angels. Men, as always,
dressed as demons. Behind the flap,
bodies writhe, contort, devour flame
& chicken heads alike. Curiosity
turns to ridicule, lust. We flesh awe
from raw human material, like kids
again, howling at all their otherness
until the otherness becomes us.

# Sovereignty

Two hundred green plastic army men circle around a tea set. All the Matchbox cars are up on blocks in the yard. While my daughter's dolls wage wars on the flamingos basking in a flagpole's swollen shadow, the mower is making birdshot of each dandelion head. For once, summer is what it seems: a trick of the light, a mistranslation, a castle of air. And all fathers are invented gods. And now I am a father, inventing a world where matchstick sailboats can set the entire ocean ablaze. My children take turns pulling me around our safe green box of earth in a red wooden wagon. It doesn't take much to convince the sky we have no idea how to hold it.

# There is No Such Thing as Trespass

Having bolt-cutted our way through
the steel mesh separating our world
from the neighbor's slightly larger
share of things, we realize nothing
here we do not already own is worth
stealing. A century compacted into
a single red silo: ours. & inside, a
mountain of uneaten grain. Ours:
three old shovels heavy with earth's
rust propping up a house that in turn
holds up one small corner of a sky.
This rain we mistake for the sky
grieving. Wet, white, bodiless dress
someone else's sister left too long on
a thin line between almond trees. &
ghosts, as always, all around us. Our
dead. Our grief. Our mother's voice
calling us home through holes built
into the fence. & this hurt: still ours.
Same empty place at our table. Same
hunger we mistake for god. Same
cross-stitch of smoke & ash working
its way up the horizon.

# A Whole New Language to Unlearn

Fire knows well what should stand
another year and what should burn.
The river that divides one country
from another times its flooding with
our divisions. It assumes struggle
unites; it hasn't always been wrong.
Pennies cover the bottom of a pond,
discolor the water, reflect, carry our
wishes down, do their best imitation
of stars. Distant rifle fire hallelujahs
the birds off an old steeple, skyward
and  away. By the time most things
learn  they're dead, we've forgotten
them, moved on, found new ways to
speak of the world so it seems more
livable. Seas bookmark continents.
Flags define the edges of belief. All
it takes is a child's paper kite to part
the sky. Sky knows the difference
between dawn and the smoky light
emanating from everyone we have
burned to try to reach it. There is no
word in this new language for birds
fleeing us, for how they hang rope-
like from a dying sky, for beauty;
how beauty will betray us someday.

# American Émigré

The fence that wrapped our field has collapsed from bolting horses & the steady weight of winter. Barbs no longer snag our jeans or bloody our hands when we flee the burning that is home. Small signal fires light the hills red. Another country some-where out there promises a peace it cannot possibly keep. Repeat after me: the cities we'll build on the ruin of other cities will shimmer & shine before they fall.

We Can Make a Home of It Still

# Another Story That Ends in Cathedral

We stopped being birds for days
after they fell. An unimaginable
sight: skies emptied of planes and
dreams, of our ownerships. Empty as
the space between our hands. At
least we remembered to love what
goes as much as what comes. Mother
had begonias and a nation growing in
her back then. My daughter was a
decade unborn. Suddenly a god for
every thirsty mouth, and I think I
remembered to love them all
equally, and forever. Even those
wingless angels amid a monsoon of
glass. Even the inferno. My father's
folded fingers arched into
conversation with the burning
moonlight flickering through a sixth
story window that overlooked stone
escarpments dropping the city off
into the Hudson. What he heard
reply from deep within the absence
the night before he leapt, unbirdlike,
isn't much use to us now, the dead or
the living.

# Homescape

I remember the land less brutal, less crowned in shotgun shells, so much less hemmed-in, shadowed, broken by birdlessness. Where a presence once passed into absence: dusky mountains. Where form reemerges: pheasants in sudden flight. I assume *from us*. I have always assumed we aren't *losing* so much as *driving away*. Let's count the seconds until our echo fades. No, not like an iron church bell leaving the air to heal itself; more like the lengthening respite between skyblaze & thunder clap. Everything I hate about what I love about home nests in this silence.

# How to Build an American House

What the saw wants once sapwood
has sung itself out. A hammer now
that all the nails are flush. A boy
after having most of his childhood
pulled from his mouth like teeth, like
song, leaving him a man. In any case,
once the job is done the thing
persists. The subject fades to object.
Its verb loses agency. *I am. At least I
am.* And the sun sinks into grass,
staining the surface red. It's good,
for now, forgetting the world keeps
going without us, that we are bright
flecks of light dancing into a back-
drop of more light. The saw hangs
static from hooks above its creation.
All the boards are in the right place.
The child has a child he hopes will
have a child someday. What is it he
wants now that the house is ready for
living?

# Privilege

A smaller holocaust was happening.
In the flooded anthill beside a raked
-apart beehive. In the summer sun's
magnification of spiders. Before the
house wore down around us, in that
misshapen light that broke through
unclasped shutters to paint odd bird-
flight on the walls. Youth's brief
ruin, before we learn to turn hurt in-
ward. Empires of salt & slug, keyed
cars, kerosene couches turned forest
fire. Before we made religion out of
ethereal things, in the body confront
-ing itself in the mirror: all acne &
sinew & scar. Pornography. Skin as
white as rock salt. When the police
drove us home again, without arrest.

# At the Wrist

Opened, & from it little wrecks fill
the tepid bathtub slowly becoming
an ocean. Every drop of us a frigate,
a war ship. Every half-meant prayer
a small city, razed: rebar & cinders:
collapsed schools, childless: plane-
loads & planeloads of smooth metal
preparing itself for piercing light.

×

Some mistakes are worth repeating,
acts that nearly erase the impotency
of being one among many. Forever
dressing & undressing into/out of
communal needs. Agency in taking
back what was never yours to give.
A stranger's life: a country warring
with itself: a body's surrender: such
slow, slow liberation.

×

Accidental hours between gesture &
forgiveness: a once-thriving battle-
field gone briefly silent. Before our
echo expires, ask all we have hurt or
meant to hurt. Our mothers, kids:
flesh, blade: ask the shadowed sky
before it heals over & forgets us.

# What My Mother Meant to Say That Night

Because men do what they want to
do, & the night just keeps skimming
quarters from the till when it thinks
no one is looking. No one is looking
when the hinged thing in my chest
swings wide & full, then empty of
itself, creaks closed forever. Of late,
alone like that, in a middle distance
between my body & another's tally
of my body, maps redrawn & walls
where a wide, lit, temporary pasture
used to be, the stars are trembling
from the weight of dreams. If *home*
is the one place we cannot return to
& *now* is the only home we'll ever
know, she tells me, how to explain
your tiny hand in mine—*home, now*
—kneading bread for your father
asleep upstairs in a half-empty bed I
half-pretend to share, how before he
wakes the waking doesn't matter, &
after I'm gone, how hungry you will
both be.

# Lesser Beasts

Breaking paper horses for the paper
pasture. Pulling all the plastic cows
from their tiny farms and leading
them, one by one, to the slaughter of
a toy chest, set ablaze at dawn. This
is how we learn the meaning of
mastery, stewardship, at such an age
for it to stick. It makes no difference
if we love our passage through this
world or if each ruin leaves a mark.
The pink ponies I've melted into a
puddle by a magnifying glass' heat
may well come back to haunt me.
My sister is already crying. Hunting
beneath the kitchen table for some-
thing to tame may mean I'll have to
rope together my father's legs and
brand him, one day. And maybe
that's okay. Animaling everything
within reach may just be part of our
nature. One could spend a lifetime
divorcing constellations from bull,
from ram, eagle, goat; from hunter
and hunted. I'm down here under an
old oak table making little beasts of
morning. The morning is crying.
Father, why is morning still crying?

# Book of the Body

When the rain grandmother's joints
prophesized refused to come & light
wore her down like an accusation, I
began to doubt the way the body
relates to its setting. How the story
moves its characters through strife/
hesitation/joy/death. How weather is
different from the storm gathering
inside. As the planes went down, I
was busy touching myself thinking
about girls I'd never speak to. Cries
entered my room from an identical
room just down a hall lined with
identical doors. When we were told
nothing would be the same, mother
was drying the dishes & readying us
for the world. When the world was
ready, we entered it. My knees hurt
from asking absence for a bit more
shape. When the shape never came,
we called it memory. When all our
memories of him grayed, we called it
ghost. When the ghost refused to
leave, we called it love. I love how
that boy's body still timidly touches
itself in an emptied bed, as if some-
one were watching, judging; how
planes continue to paint shadows up
& up & down my wall, as if we live
in that story anymore.

# July the 4ᵗʰ

We're lying down in a buzzcut field
watching gut-shot night sparkle &
shower us all in a hot fizzled glow.
Hiding inside ourselves as children
unsure how a country works. Rifts
excised for an hour. The distraction
of  awe. Watching miniature flags
flap fiercely on thin plastic sticks.
Even the statues are forgetting their
lost battles. Moss is forgetting how
to hold the stone walls in place. *So
much blue up there,* our daughter
says. *& reds, but together.*

# Valentine

The love note wet in my hand; ink erasing itself. The girl is nowhere I'd know how to find her. Moved on or dead. The news on grandpa's old transistor warns that those of us still here should stay indoors for the forseeable future. He admits the future after that is unforeseen. Thick moss brailles up the white picket schoolyard fence. Some newly discovered planet, he boasts, & another that is merely a moon. The principal talks about reinstating the drill. My father says his father never forgot the calm gray expressions on those he killed. There is a box banded to each desk. I have no idea which of us deserves this love.

# Grace Notes

We are driving west with the sun
swaddled in storm cloud and all that
pristine nothingness that is Kansas
flattening behind us. I've learned
there are ways to sing along to radio
silence, though I'm less convinced
these days anyone is listening. How
quickly winter empties our voices of
their animals; windows down and
the gray horizon suddenly too small
to carry inside. You are the worst
kind of lover: highway, landlocked
between fled and imagined homes.
As our headlights like slowly falling
fires kick out into the afternoon rain
and the kids from the backseat start
naming everything that blurs by us
birds and, suddenly birds again, we
begin making Motown of the dead
air. I have no idea what I promised
them about tomorrow, but the sky is
devastating as whirling white asters.
And no clouds will ever make these
wild animal shapes again.

# Dear Noah

There is no boat big enough to un-
ruin, no flood more violent than our
own. Like a ghost haunted by itself,
we move along old scars terrified of
what would happen if left to heal. A
blast in Kabul last night: six bodies,
three children. Walls are being built
along the southern lip of a country
right now, as we speak. What else
would it sound like if not godvoice,
threat undercut with enough hope to
slip an ark through. I cannot blame
you anymore for tracing your finger
over imagined horizons. My brother
returned home husked & empty. So
many papers collect on our rickety
porch. Even Everest is underwater.

# How We All Came to be Here

Paperclips laced into wagon train. Cotton balls swab a cardboard sky. Matchstick men, women, & tiny toy children readying their future fires. Wire hangers, stained blue, trace the river's current out to sea. Of course, there's no sea in this model: it's 1986, a week before a space shuttle would shatter our dreams of flight & a few hours after my first kiss & right around the time my father told me *When you can't make them see the light, make them feel the heat*, & my school project exists in an Idaho too long ago to make sense of. Who knew wild endless waters were only two map inches away? & popsicle sticks stand in for rifles & arrows. A lattice of red yarn follows both their trajectories. Each horse is a brown paper bag stretched over toothpicks. A few oxen will make it through the day. Flecks of green tissue consume the rest.

# Fallow as That

We are out divining fish from dried riverbeds again. Going through all the appropriate motions, like prayer. Even before our hands are strong enough to hold it, guide its tautness through our fragile fingers, making sure nothing snaps, someone passes us some wire woven around a pole and demands we pull the world up by the mouth. So much later will come the rifles, flags, and crosses. But it takes time to learn to give up on ourselves. Today we are running our lines along an arid crust of earth as if the future depends on us. Back and forth, clicking our tongues, deer in the near distance, just as hungry.

# Errata

Between evergreens, as if animals at
dusk jostling by a lakebed for that
first taste of still russet water. Better
yet, broad stones carved into stairs
scattered throughout the overgrown
understory, leading nowhere. Love
feels out of context among so many
dead & thirsting things. Strike that;
love has always been a great sorrow
sated only by the greater sorrows of
others. That we are here at all seems
~~miraculous fated chance agency~~. As
if waiting for beauty to come along &
perfect us. Then strike perfection.
Strike out at idealized beauty. & at
the animals we look like scrambling
around these cities we've built atop
~~permanent~~ older cities. When I say
we're animals, at best I mean we are
home. For *river*, read *the numbness
of night trickling down our throats*.
When I said *stairs*, I never meant
~~heaven~~ thank you.

# Salvage

*Delray, Detroit, 2014*

From this fourth story window I see
powerlines eating sky, gray awnings
blocking all light from the recesses.
All neon-like; the entirety of night is
captured, drowned in inch-deep
puddles. A child half-buried in tarp,
asleep between walls. Walls buried
up to their necks in empty shelves.
Overabundance of place. & scarcity
of the same. Self-interrogations. Sag
& soot. A man older than my father
was when he died is converting fire
hydrants to Jesus. & it seems to be
working; amen. No fire has stuck
around long enough to catch. There
is a boarded-up church just out of
reach, a weed-choked stone temple
that can't shake off its steeple. Like
soggy piñatas, stars just hang there,
slashed open, all the sweetness torn
out. Like a barren womb. Like some
-thing we must learn the worth of
through trial & error. Like waiting
for a god or steamroller to speak up
and rephrase us.

# Places We Visit Once, & Never Again

Not the whole house, just the bed-
room where a dead boy still has not
quite died. Humming from posters,
trophies, within the seashells lining a
window that has never overlooked
an ocean. Not the entire river either,
just its shore, that drowning half of
the tide. It's not that we don't miss
the field, where the farmhands pray
for rain to stop, then pray pray pray
for it to rain again. But let's skip the
storm part next time. The thirst, its
prayers. After my father dragged me
to Gettysburg when I was twelve &
told me to *look, really look* I knew
we'd never return. Not from that.
Next time let's dig a hole the size of
a child & set a small fire inside &
move two counties away & see if it
is true what they say about wounds.
Instead of just his room, let's leave
the whole house to echo by itself.

# There Was No Heaven

There in the lightning-leaving, once
silence has taken hold & those idiot
yellow birds return to the high elms.
Church bells unstiffen, clash again.
The clouds disbanding so swiftly I
almost mistake them for love. Those
aren't bits of star caught in rewind,
son; the sky has been zipped & un-
zipped too often to know what light
has always been here & what lights
are just now igniting. Fading. Yes,
that means the eternity within us is
shortening. No, pinesmoke is a sign
& is not a sign & I don't know what
for. & if you count the receding
seconds between clap & flash, yes
my boy, you can calculate precisely
when the sky will close back up.

# Field Sermon: Renunciation

If the cut is clean, a cross-sectioned
sky reveals the same spent rings as
ponderosa pine. Inside our body's
body, when turned to music, a cry so
close to song. And the lake filled
with men in white finding some sort
of grace in the silt is the same spot
my dad once taught me how to gut
walleye. Blood in the shallows. God
along the mirrored surface. Listen
closely, that distant clamor of belled
goats may be the great gale grandpa
always said would blow the whole
house down. To bring the dead back
to us, never speak of them again.

# The Children

If you fear it, child, fear it until risk
wears itself down to certainty: until
the monsters you've imagined under
your bed resemble your father, your
neighbor, your hands: until country
betrays its *otherness*.

×

No more fireworks or unseen strikes
of lightning. Those aren't offseason
hunters or trucks bellowing into the
not-so-distant night. Come here; let
me hold you like a candle holds its
heat. You are old enough to name
things as they are.

×

Spiderwebbed across your bedroom
window, cracks that gently ease into
shatter. Shatter, into enter. A cold
winter wind makes the flame dance,
sputter & snuff. Smoke that cannot
possibly be exhaust. I won't tell you
how enter eventually eases into exit.

×

No, not yet; let me hold you

×

like this for a few more minutes: like a
world, reducing: like how the
displaced still hold to home.

# Three Ways to Feign Suicide

The neon interrupting night calls us.
Behind the only convenience store in
this town built on convenience,
safety, hall monitors, & bright white
fences, we exhaust our bodies. Un-
labeled pills, vodka, screwing what-
ever recognizes itself in the swollen
whiteness of our eyes. It's not the
dying, not *how*, but the uncertain
*whenness*. That we may all be loved
like good little sons, but not equally.

×

There are a thousand ways to say it,
but we'll take touching ourselves or
each other over *the world will never
be more than the world* any day. As
we sketch schools in dust with our
heels, call our dead older brothers
*teacher*, burn our returned letters to
god. As we love like unconquered
trees, like hay in horseless fields. As
we yell *fire* in crowded fires, press
twigs to our temples to mean *bang*.

×

It's not the glue holding broken toys
together but that anyone bothered. It
is no bother, sparrow, hurling stones
at you when our candles burn longer
than our hands can hold them. Each
day is the day the earth ends, & then
there's always tomorrow. Morning
needles through night to find us no

closer or farther from ourselves; all
our kicked-out-of-heavenness gone.
What I think I mean to say is, we're
just animal enough to stay.

# Northernmost November

Say the town is an oil-stained rag.
Call each body a ball-peen hammer
doing everything it can to make
things flush again; the raw coming
apart-together-apart of floorboards
as winter tightens the grains into
fists. I follow the blanketing bird
flight with my index finger bent like
a trigger, still nothing plummets. I
have no say in migration, or how
quickly ice will thaw. Some of us
must stay behind to witness. Say
there is something worth witnessing
in an emptied sky. Say the dead help
us wrap ourselves around life. This
absence of animals hurts more than a
hallway of old photographs. I hope it
never stops hurting. I hope we'll
keep beating our bodies into each
other long after the birds have
returned. Let's decide to call this
love. At least an honest attempt at
loving what remains. Next time I
point my finger at the sky, say all the
stars will shatter and rain down their
light. Say that light is already in us.

# Toy Boat

*for a friend*

There is no this or that body, only
embrace or escape. I understand the
slow song nooses make in a motel
room at night. I'm not immune to a
sleep empty of nightmares, empty of
arms demanding you love some
things more than others, of unhealed
exit wounds and munitions and all
that goes along with remaining here.
That toy boat once larger than all
seven continents barely fits the old
ceramic ocean in the back yard. I
know nothing our mothers foretold
came true: the horizon at dawn is just
an x-ray of a shattered spinal cord,
and only the dead can be born again.
Our bodies are sixty percent water; I
understand that's not enough to
drown in. We have rivers for that
kind of thing. Undertows. Pills and
the solace of a warm bath. There is
no lesser dark, Doug. Where they
burn longest, stars only stress the rest
of night. All boats are plastic, for a
time. There are no oceans, no
promises to keep or rescind. The
children we thought would never die
in us were never really children. I
hope we are found to have lived
without illusion, sailed without
wind.

# Reparations

Maybe not for the dead exactly,
more their silenced echoes. How air
skates each prayer over a raw body
of earth without penetrating. For all
those migrant hands sunk between
nations. A palmful of plums, apples;
a lungful of coal. How our short-
lived bodies act as insurrections;
sometimes, consolations. For dying
unions; the hesitant oaths mothers
make to their uniformed sons from
docks that end in clean gray ships.
For how frantically they wave; how
full their emptying arms. This is for
that fullness. For the gods it took to
get us this far and the gods we'd kill
or invent for just one more breath.
I have failed you again; and this is for
that failing. For the wailing we think
should shake the earth, that changes
nothing. I was wrong; this has
always been for the dead. And I have
risked so little to linger here.

# Previous Winners of The Orison Poetry Prize

Carly Joy Miller, *Ceremonial* (2018)
Selected by Carl Phillips

Rebecca Aronson, *Ghost Child of the Atalanta Bloom* (2017)
Selected by Hadara Bar-Nadav

J. Scott Brownlee, *Requiem for Used Ignition Cap* (2016)
Selected by C. Dale Young

# ABOUT THE AUTHOR

John Sibley Williams is the author of the poetry collections *Skin Memory* (Backwaters Prize, forthcoming 2019), *Disinheritance*, and *Controlled Hallucinations*. He serves as the editor of *The Inflectionist Review* and has edited two Northwest poetry anthologies, *Alive at the Center* (Ooligan Press, 2013) and *Motionless from the Iron Bridge* (barebones books, 2013). Williams is the winner of numerous literary awards, including the Laux/Millar Prize, the Philip Booth Award, the *American Literary Review* Poetry Contest, the Phyllis Smart-Young Prize, the 46er Prize, the Nancy D. Hargrove Editors' Prize, the *Confrontation* Poetry Prize, and the *Vallum* Award for Poetry. He lives in Portland, Oregon with his partner, twin toddlers, and a voracious Boston Terrier.

# ABOUT ORISON BOOKS

Orison Books is a 501(c)3 non-profit literary press focused on the life of the spirit from a broad and inclusive range of perspectives. We seek to publish books of exceptional poetry, fiction, and non-fiction from perspectives spanning the spectrum of spiritual and religious thought, ethnicity, gender identity, and sexual orientation.

As a non-profit literary press, Orison Books depends on the support of donors. To find out more about our mission and our books, or to make a donation, please visit www.orisonbooks.com.